Conceptualism
~Mind, Body & Art!~

Written by

Chavanese Wint

 New Generation Publishing

This book is dedicated to those individuals who cannot see beyond their vision in the future, those individuals who have never stopped dreaming, to those individuals who keeps fighting for their dreams, life and success. To those of you who are always surrounded by negativity, people who have come into your life to stop your **creativity**, but *I* believe in you, YES! You have the ability. If you seek inspiration to never give up, to never stop fighting for your dreams, goals and your success, **then, this book is for YOU!**

CONTENTS

'IT'

Time: 20:59
Date: 28.7.2015

~

*People who say **'IT'** cannot be done;
Should <u>never</u> **interfere** with others who are doing **IT**.*

When you say **'IT',** cannot be **done**,
Already in my mind, I have **won**,
I have just shot you, with my positive **gun,**
Now, your **negative** words have come **undone**.

~

~Whatever I want in my **life,**
I will **work,** and I will **fight**,
That means, it is not up to you to **choose it**.~

So, if you carry on with your **negativity**,
To stop my **creativity**,
I can **promise** you today, you will <u>lose</u> it.

~

My creativity to succeed,
Should only depend on how I breathe
My willingness depends, on how I achieved it.

So when you tell me "I'm a **failure",
I've already got the best job in **Australia**,
You need to stop that **negative behaviour**,
Because, I will not stop praying to my **saviour**.**

I am in Charge!
Time: 00:19
Dated: 29.7.2015

~

I am **in charge** of how I feel,
And today, I am choosing _happiness_.

I will not be **depressed**,
I will learn the life, of **togetherness**,
Forgetting about the **sadness**,
And start to fill that void, of **loneliness**.

~

I've _realised,_ that my sins are something that I need to
confess,
In order for me to move on, I must try a little **tenderness**.

I must work a little harder, if I want to see the path to
success,
I will give it all I can, but never settle for **second best**.

~

I know sometimes, I might start to feel a little **suppressed**,
But, all I have to do, is close my eyes, and take a **rest**.

I will do the best I can, and choose my own **happiness**,
I can feel my life **changing**, there is no more **sadness*****

Intelligence
Time: 03:01
Date: 26.7.2015

Intelligence without **ambition,** is like a bird without **wings,**
And can you **imagine** a bird not flying; as **beautifully** as it
sings?

~

Intelligence is one of the most **passionate** and most
amazing **things,**
To have *intelligence*, is like playing a guitar, without
strings.

**The sexiest man, will open your legs,
While a handsome man, will open your eyes,
A gentleman, will open your heart,
But, an intelligent man, will open your mind.**

~

At times, it is better to be kind than right,
It's like leading the blind to stand, in their own light.

We sometimes need an *intelligent* mind that **speaks,**
But, having a **patient** heart, will never go **unseen**.

Respecting Sally
Time: 04:30
Date: 29.7.2015

Respect yourself enough to walk away from anything that
no longer serves you,
Grows you,
Or makes you **happy**.

~

Why be in a **negative relationship when you know that
it is **crappy**?**

~Now, come on, **Sally**,
Everyone knows that he treats you bad, and you are
unhappy,
You are having babies with him; just to change the **nappy**.~

~

He beats you,
He puts you **down**,
What are the **lessons** of love, that you have **found**?

**~He has stolen your queen's crown,
Now, in that love river, you have drowned.~**

~

*****Respecting** yourself may take a lot of **courage**,
It is not basic science, but it will take a lot of
knowledge.***

***It's like a _single mother;_ working her **hardest** to go
back to **college**,

4

She's not thinking about the father of her child,
She's not being **discouraged**,
She's thinking about the future, and how she is going to
flourish.***

~

So **respecting** yourself might be a little hard,
But, once you have over-come this, you will always go far.

~There is no man on earth that should make you **unhappy**,
You have a bright future ahead; please listen to me,
Sally.~

Comfort Zone

Time: 01:56
Date: 3.1.2017

It's time for you to get out of your **comfort zone,**
I don't want to hear the bullshit, I don't want to hear **moans**,
All I want is for you to start switching off all your **phones**,
Because at the end of this sentence you will be **mind
blown**.

~

So you say you want **success**, but I should leave you alone,
I should give up on your ass, let you make it **alone**,
But let me teach you this, no one ever gains success on
their **own**,
So if you want to act tough, bitch, I am more **fully grown**.

Been in the game in and out, sleeping on benches all **alone**,
Wrapping up on my blanket, because I wanted to leave
home,
Yes I thought that I knew IT all, yes I thought I was **grown**,
But deep inside I was empty, living like the **unknown**.

~

Every flesh on my body, every blood even **bones**,
Wanted success and all the money, I wanted to sit on the
throne,
So I worked my ass off, stepped over every single **stone**,
Now, I've got the books, all the cars, never had to take out
a **loan**.

Don't you think that I wanted to call my daddy on the **phone**?
Wanted to cry my eyes out, wanted to go back **home**,
Wanted the hugs and all the kisses that I've always been
shown,
But I thought no fuck that; girl, get that money **alone**.

~

Don't be **misguided**, be tough, have a strong **backbone**,
If you want to be a singer then pick up that **microphone**,
But don't you think you know it all, because you will end
up **alone**,
Please listen before you speak, come here, smell my **cologne**.

Success!!!

Surround Yourself

Time: 18:47
Date: 28.7.2015

Surround yourself with the **dreamers** and the **doers,**
The **believers** and the **thinkers,**
But, most of all, surround yourself with, **YOU!**

~

You have the _TALENT_ to **succeed;
You're not **faithless**, GO, **proceed**,
Never be **aimless,** and you will not **bleed**,
Just be **painless**, even when life is not **guaranteed.****

When you _believe_ in yourself, you will amount to
something **great.**
You're a **dreamer** and a **doer,** so just forget about the **hate.**

~

Forget about the **diamonds and the _babies,_ just have **faith**,
If you **believe** in yourself, you could become the next
president of the **United States.****

~You are **strong,**
You are **powerful**,
But, don't you sit around and **wait,**
Don't be _sitting_ around thinking, that your dreams can just
create.~

~

You have to _fight,_ you have to **choose,**
Yes, a _thinker_ will sometimes **lose,**
But when a **_dreamer_** falls and gets back up, he will never
have the **blues.**

8

Negativity
Time: 18:22
Date: 28.7.2015

~

Don't expect to see **positive** changes in your life if you surround yourself with **negative** people.

*You will eat,
Sleep,
Shit,
Speak,
Break the rules like _negativity_ is equal.*

~

_Because _negativity_ is evil._

You don't want to be down in the **dumps**,
Smoking weed,
Taking pills,
Drinking alcohol like it is legal.

~

You want to be around **positivity**,
Using your brain to create **productivity**,
Making money and flying like an Eagle.

Now listen **people**,
Negativity is wrong, YES, it is **lethal**.

~

Don't be around party people,
The womanisers and the booty shakers,
Because those are the ones using the needles.

They will pull you in **everyday**,
pretending to smile, not **pray**,
While behind your back they are out there being **deceitful**.

~

Now, I know *negativity* can sometimes be fun,
It can make you **laugh**, **sing** and act **gleeful**.

But, this is **life**,
This is **real**,
People will go out there and **steal**,
And those are the ones attending the wrong **cathedrals**.

Tough People

Time: 03:38
Date: 29.7.2015

***Tough times don't last,
Only tough people do.***

~

Life is a **challenge**,
But, you will have to see it **through**.

~*Life* is a **battle**,
It will kick you, until you are blue,
But, once you're **successful**, you will have the **greatest
view**.

~

Tough times will look you in the face and say,
"HEY! I know you **cannot** do it,"
But, you're strong enough to know, that it's your **dream,**
and you will **pursue** it.

So, never let **tough times get you **down**,
Hardship is what you've always **knew**,
Just work a little harder to **succeed**,
And you will be sipping on your **brew**.**

Winners

Time: 23:26
Date: 25.7.2015

~

Winners,* are not people who never **fail,
Winners, are people who never quit.**

Winners, are not people who gives up on their **dreams**,
Winners, are people who fight, even when they are **sick**.

~

~So please take your **pick**,
It's either **destruction,** or a lifetime full of **failure**,
You can live it like this, but it won't work in your **favour**.~

You can **steal**, **rob**, **kill** or **abuse**,
That *needle* in your hand, will only be **used**.

~

You can stop for a moment, take sometime to **rethink**,
Just brush your shoulders off, and take a bath in that **sink**.

Mistakes are proof, that you are really trying **harder**,
Choose the right path now, before you're backed up in that
corner.**

Success

Time: 02:40
Date: 24.7.2015

~

Success isn't about what you have **accomplished** in your
life,
It's about what you do to **inspire** others.

Taking them away from the **crack cocaine,
Inspiring them to use their **brains**,
While helping them to choose the right path,
And ensuring that you decrease their **pains.** **

~

Success is about the path and the **journey** that you take,
Spreading the works of God, and never being **fake**.

Success is about the life that you have lived,
Inspiring others, without gaining a thing.

~

***Success** is about gaining **knowledge**,
From a lawyer to a doctor, attending the right **college**.**

Success, is about the person that you are,
Your intentions to _succeed_,
And the **will power,** to go far.

~

Success isn't about showing off your diamond rings,
Making others feel lonely, while you move on to the next
best thing.******

Success is about believing in yourself,
Having the **faith** to proceed, while you work harder for
your **wealth**.

~

Success is about living all your **dreams**,
To look past all the **difficulties**,
And to **realise** that the world is not as hard as it may **seem.**

Positive Message
Time: 23:09
Date: 25.7.2015

Work hard in **silence**, and let **success** be your **noise**,
If you **desire** to make it in the **future**, you have to put
away your **toys**.

~

*__Life__ isn't a game,
There might be no **tomorrow**,
__Fight__ for what you want,
And never think about the **sorrows**.*

Ambition, is one of the paths to **success**,
Motivation, is what needs to come next,
Determination, **determines** your own **destination**,
With all of these words, might lead to **frustration**.

~

*So remember, do not shout and come across all **aggressive**,
Your **future** starts here, so please listen to this **message**.*

Persistence
Time: 12:28
Date: 25.1.2013

~

In life, you have to learn about **persistence**,
Dedication and **determination,** is built in your **existence**.

I know you feel **afraid**,
But, it's good to be **consistent**,
Just work real hard, and don't you think about the **distance**.

~

If you put in the **hard work,**
Results might not come in an **instance**,
But, if you change your **mind frame,** it is all about
acceptance.

*Don't worry about the world, they will change their
appearance
But, you will always be the same, so please remember,
resistance.*

~

If you need some help, then call an **assistant**,
But never give up **hope**, just remember, **consistent**.

*It's like a little baby boy, growing up into an **infant**,
He will crawl real **slowly**, then you will really start to see
the **difference**.*

It's OK
Time: 01:32
Date: 24.7.2015

It's OK if you didn't grow up with a **diaper** made out of
dollar **bills**,
Just focus on your dreams, and you'll be living in the **hills**.

~

It's OK if your mama was just always taking **pills**,
You are **talented,** you are **gifted**, please, just focus on
your **skills**.

It's OK if you're living in Africa and sleeping in boarded
houses,
You are **human**, not a **victim**, forget about those **mouses**.

~

It's OK if you have no money and you are really trying to
make it,
Don't put yourself down, because **negativity** will surely
break it.

It's OK to fight for your dreams, and to know where you
are **going**,
Even if they tell you that your life is fucking **boring**.

~

It's OK to have faith in the simplest **things**,
Just keep waiting on that phone call, God will surely make
it **ring**.

Ambitions
Time: 00:30
Date: 26.7.2015

~

Take a **look** in the **mirror**,
Do you see that **person**?
That's your only **competition.**

That **desire**,
That **drive**,
It should be your only *ambition*.

~

To have *ambition* is **priceless**,
It is born within your **veins**,
You will **strive** to **succeed**, and don't you think about the
pain.

Ambition, is about having **enthusiasm**,
It's a **purpose** to **fight**,
It's a **purpose** to keep on going,
So that you can see the **light**.

~

Ambition is **persistence**,
A chance to work harder for your **goals**,
That **passion**,
That **strength**,
To see what noone else **knows**.

Without *ambition*, we are empty,
And our **dreams** might never come to **light**,
We will never believe in ourselves, **day** or **night**.

Something Meaningful
Time: 1:30
Date: 26.7.2015

If you want to **succeed as bad as you want to **breathe**,
Then you will become **successful**.**

~

Success contains a lot of **things** ,
And one of those words are **stressful**.

You have to wake up **everyday**,
Make a **plan**, then you **pray**,
But never you be **forgetful**.

~

You have the **determination,
The **drive**,
The **motivation,** to **strive**,
But most of all, you have the **potential**.**

As you go through life, you will meet a lot of people,
So never you be **disrespectful**.

~

You have to find a **team**,
Something **strong**,
Someone **clean**,
__Don't__ pay **attention** to those who are out there being
judgemental.

Now as you fight for your **success,
You might end up in a **mess**,
So always keep the important things **confidential**.**

Imma

Time: 01:20
Date: 3.1.2017

They say the sky is the limit,
But I see further than **that**.

Imma dress up in my clothes, Imma put on my **hat**,
I'm gonna show the world that I will succeed, no time to sit
down and **chat**,
Imma fight for what I want, get a house and move out of
my **flat**.

I don't care if you are out there thinking you're **fat**,
You can lose all that weight girl, give that batty a **slap**.

I ain't got nine lives, like that beautiful **cat**,
But Imma spread my wings and fly around, be like a **Bat**.

And when I wake up one day, Imma do a big **spat**,
I've made my mark in the world, God, look at all **that**.

Imma hold my head up high, but never behave like a **brat**,
Then at the end of my journey, Imma brush my shoulders
off and give it a **pat**.

Your Love
Time: 03:32
Date: 26.7.2015

~

Your love is like an **umbilical cord,**
It's like I was **attached** to you by birth,
Then got chopped off with a **sword.**

Every night I pray to God, I've even asked his son, the
Lord,
For him to bring you back to me,
These are the words, that I have taped **record.**

~

He told me not to worry, has my *faith* is being **restored**,
But losing you once again, is a <u>*destruction*</u> that I cannot
afford.

Now, I don't know what to do with my **life**,
What am I working **towards**?
I am here looking for you out of this window,
And I am starting to feel **bored.**

~

I thought that love always had a **reward**,
I loved you with every **bone** in my body,
But now my blood is being **poured.**

They told me to move on,
Live life,
The <u>*world*</u> is something that I am yet to **explore.**

21

~

But, how can I move on, when you are not here?
I am sorry, I can't, you are someone that I've always
adored.

Negative People
Time: 19:19
Date: 28.7.2015

Avoid **negative** people,
For they are the greatest *destroyers* of the world.

~

The destroyers of motivation,
The destroyers of determination,
The destroyers for you, working towards your goals.

They are the *destroyers* of **self confidence**,
The destroyers of **self esteem,**
The *destroyers* that were made, build to **shatter dreams.**

~

~A *machine* that is made out of **lies**,
Negativity will **kill,** and it will **fight**,
It will break you, until you are made of bones.~

Its flesh is like the **devil**,
Making trouble, like a **rebel**,
It's the greatest, it wears a **medal**.

~

So let's trade,
Negativity, or your life,
Please choose wisely, remember your wife.

This is your future, it is not a **dream**,
Things aren't as easy, as they may **seem**,
This is not a life made out of **creams**,
I can see your body floating, in the river **stream.**

Homelessness
Time: 00:38
Date: 25.4.2015

~

Did you know that there are many people suffering from
homelessness?
No *food* to eat, nothing to *drink;* they are **motionless.**

~They have no roof, no home, they are full of **loneliness,**
But here you are, talking about **hopelessness.**~

~

You say that you are **grateful,**
But you are filled with a lot of **coldness,**
You've got your *mum,* you've got *a dad*,
But, you can't spell ***forgiveness***.

Those people out there, their bodies are the definition of
brokenness,
But, dear God, please cover them with all your **holiness.**

~

All we can do is fight the battle with **openness,**
Forget the *drugs,* forget the *crack*, DREAM; never become
defenceless.

Your **willingness** to *succeed*, should be full of **boldness,**
But, no *aggression,* no more hate, THINK, **happiness.**

24

Negative Thoughts
Time: 21:59
Date: 28.7.2015

STOP! You're thinking about what might go **wrong**,
Let's start thinking about what WILL go **right**.

~

Do you know how bad it feels when _negativity_ **bites?**
It burns into your blood like a snake being **uptight**.

** It **wriggles** and it **moves**,
It is not a good **delight**,
When it burns into your **veins**, that's its way of being
polite. **

~

~So let's start thinking about the **positives**,
Let's think about the **MIGHTS**;
Let's think about the **positivity**, starting to come to **light**.~

***It is easier to think about the **could have beens**,
The **probabilities**,
And the **NOTS**.***

~

But when we think about the **HAVE TOO**
The **MAYBES** and the **BUTS**,
Our life will start to **MOULD**, and that's when **positivity**
will start to **POP**.

Behind Her Lipstick

Time: 06:13
Date: 7.5.2015

There's something about her *smile*, and I am trying to read all the **clues,**
It looks so pretty, but her lipstick is blue.

~

Pour me a glass of **brew,**
This *situation* here, has to be **untrue,**
I see so much pain, and I am all the way, in the back of the **queue.**

So let's see if this is **true.**
When she was younger, her father used to beat her with a **screw,**
Then at the age of 15, she then started sniffing **glue.**

~

Her *smile* tells me that she had lost her little **shoe,**
She had no clothing just a dress, and she loved it, it was blue.

Her mummy picked it out for her, before she started on the **glue,**
Before all the **crack and drugs**, it was her and her baby brother, she loved him **too.**

~

~ But, she had to grow up faster,
This was something she always **knew,**
Taking care of her little brother, while her dreams she had
to **pursue.** ~

~

So yeah, no one really knows, NO, they haven't got a **clue,**
But they judge her by her lip stick, all because it is blue.

As I stand here looking, her beauty has a wonderful **view,**
I know that I'm a stranger, but I am crying with **you.**

~

Don't worry, you will see this **through.**
All your struggles as an ending, it will be a very successful
view.

Oh hi, I'm an author, that blue lipstick looks lovely on **you,**
She holds her nose and sneezes, yes my beauty, may God
bless you...

Foundation

Time: 00:44
Date: 3.1.2017

****Difficult roads only lead to beautiful destinations,
Stay strong and be focused, let's build a foundation.****

You ain't got a job? Let's start those **applications**,
I know that it's been hard, but you need to lose that
frustration.
That weed, oh that crack, all those fucking **temptations**,
It's time to make that money girl, start your **calculations**.

Breathe, stretch fuck those **accusations**,
You're talented you will succeed, show them haters your
demonstration.

Yes I know that you can do it, it's all about the **dedication**,
Get that suit and put it on, now start your **meditation**,
It's now time for you to get out of this **situation**,
And I promise in the end, you'll get a big **celebration**.

Success is the key, but you need to be **patient**,
Rome wasn't build in a day, yes it had some **complications**,
And let those haters out there laugh like it is an
hallucination,
You've got your eyes on your goals girl, yes, you've built
that **foundation**.

More Open
Time: 04:51
Date: 29.7.2015

She said,
"I am down in the dumps, and I am **broken**.

~

"All those years of **abuse**,
All those years of **drug use**,
I have never once stood up and **spoken**.

"But, I am tired of this **life**,
I am tired, of the **cries**,
I am ready to **slap** myself and be **awoken**.

~

"I was always wearing a **frown** because my *dreams* were
choking.
When I was a child I was **abused**,
Yes, I know I was a **fool**,
But, my *innocence* never had to be **taken**.

"My mother **used** me like a **tool**,
I couldn't stand up on a **stool**,
She **mistreated** me like I was a worthless dirty **token**.

~

"And if you think that I am full of **lies**,
The result is in my **cries**,
I don't really care if you think that I am **joking**.
I am standing up for all the women who need to be more
outspoken.

~

"Don't let **abuse** get to **you**,
I know you've felt pain **too**,
But, it helps to change a life, when you are **open**."

Her Feelings
Time: 05:14
Date: 7.5.2015

~

~You'll be **amazed** to know what happens behind **closed
doors**,
All the **beatings**,
All the **crying**,
Even **killings** and more.~

<u>Certain</u> people give up **hope**,
They are broken down for **sure**,
That pretty **youthful** look, is no longer **adored**.

~

This situation here, got her feeling so **unsure**,
So she turned to the **booze**, down at the **convenience store.***

She's **fretting**, she's a **mess**,
And her throat is getting **sore**,
She sips a little more to forget being **insecure**.

~

31

But, she's a **mother**,
No **STOP**! She cannot take it **anymore**,
All this moving, she has no **status**,
This is so fucked up, for sure.

She stares at her cigar,
Then she looks to the door,
She wants to make a run for it,
But, she would only drop to the floor.

~

She **looks** at her **daughter**,
Yeah, she's ageing now for sure.

And in that moment,
She only wished,
She had it all, then maybe,
Their relationship could be **restored**.

Women

Time: 01:25
Date: 30.4.2015

Women, they are **smarter** than you think they are,
But, not nearly as smart as they think *they*are.

~

~ They will leave you to **think**,
Maybe, even give you a second **blink**,
But, if mess up again, they will make you **shrink**,
Watching you closely, as they're *sipping* on their **drink**. ~

Cheat all you want,
Some will cry, or even **sink**,
But, they will put themselves **back together**,
Then move slowly, on the **brink**.

~

So maybe it's time for you to **rethink**.
They will **take care** of you,
They will **cook**,
Even wash up, over the kitchen **sink**.

~ But, playing with their hearts,
will have you swimming in **red ink**. ~

~

Because, they're strong enough to know,
When a ***cheater,*** is doing a ***lip sync***.

I Know
Time: 02:09
Date: 24.7.2015

There is no **elevator to **success**,
You have to take the **stairs**,
life is a **journey**, so you have to wipe away those **tears**.**

~

I know that it's been **difficult**,
I have seen it all these years,
All the **struggles**, all the **hardship**, YES!,
They've murdered all your **peers**.

**But life doesn't end there, you have to keep your
head held high,
Fight those battles and believe in yourself; GO! Give
the world a try.**

~

~ As long as you are living, and not just some **bones** that
has just **died**,
life is a **journey**, go, hop on, *give it a try*. ~

What About Me?
Time: 02:00
Date: 27.4.2015

~

She said,
"You're **not** even _thinking_ of me,
Your only way of _thinking_, is if you go on a **drinking spree**,
Now, leave me be.

"You're my **mother**, but my feelings you **cannot see,**
Yes, I know that you are both my **parents**, when my
father decided to **flee**.

~

"But it wasn't up to **me**,
Take **responsibility** for your daughter who needs
protection, guaranteed.

_**"All I do is help you,
Only to cry under a tree**_.

~

"I cannot call my **uncle**,
I _cannot_ call my **aunty**,
No, no, I can't, no, I cannot call **Marie**.

"I just want to let this go, so I can finally be **free**,
Marry a husband, who would never **leave**, or ever
forsaken me.

~

35

*"I'll be **happy**,*
*I'll be **joyful**,*
*I'll be swimming in the **sea**.*

~

"Oneday when I am gone,
You'll regret, that you never took care of **me**."

Devotion

Time: 04:22
Date: 29.7.2015

~

** You can't kill someone, who already has dead **emotions**.
Someone who's heart is **trapped**, **shattered** and **thrown**
into the **ocean**. **

~ You cannot turn around and say "you are taking away
your **devotions**",
When deep down you know, your love is stronger than a
potion. ~

~

She **loves** you,
She **cares**,
Why do you think she's starting a **commotion**?

When you ignore all the *__signs__*,
That's when things will blow up, like an **explosion**.

~

**If you love her very much, then you should watch her
body **motions**,
Spend some quality time with her, and start applying that
love **lotion**.**

When she gives you her **heart**, you don't just tear it to **pieces**,
You cannot lift her up, then break her down, as it **pleases**.

~

~ A women's mind is filled with a **combination** of **love** and **lust**,
There is so much they can take, until they start to feel **mistrust**. ~

Bad Mother

Time: 00:50
Date: 27.4.2015

She said,
"I feel like calling my **friend** right now,
Or maybe, I should call my **uncle**?
God knows that I am so **broken** right now,
God knows, I feel like I am gonna **crumble**.

~

"I can't live my life like this anymore,
I can't take it, when you are drunken,
You need to realise that you are older now,
You are not some monkey in a jungle.

"You are my ***mother***, and I know that we have been
through **struggles**,
But, your **drunkenness** always gets you into **troubles**.

~

"I **can't** do this anymore, so it's time I start to **give up**,
I will *leave* you to drink, all that **alcohol**, out of your
cup…"

Drinking Mummy
Time: 01:37
Date: 27.4.2015

~

~ Two bottles of **alcohol** a **night**,
You drink everyday, when you should be **holding** me **tight**. ~

Your **aggression** is so **deep**,
You're causing **mean-less fights**,
When are you ever, going to see the **light**?

~

You're so **uptight**,
You always think that you're forever in the **right**,
When you **consume** so much **alcohol**, you will lose your
eyesight.

Look at your **height**,
You're so small, but think that you're a bloody sweet
delight.

~

* But, you're **nothing**.
Just a mother, who will **never** see the **light**,
Now go, hope you **sleep tight**. *

The Seeds

Time: 23:21
Date: 23.7.2015

~

~The <u>seeds</u> that you plant today have a great **potential** to
harvest in many years to **come**,
If you only think about where you are **going**, and what you
are doing **wrong**.~

Stop that **noise**, you are **strong**.
I see **depression**, I see pain, but they are **wrong**,
You will **overcome** this feeling, use your faith, go sing
your **songs**.

~

*I knew all **along**,
You will achieve amazing things, because you are
strong.*

You're determined,
You're educated,
You'll be off to **Hong Kong.**

~

**And when the devil tries to win, just laugh and say, you
are **wrong**.
I'm a woman of Christ, and today, is how my life **began**.**

The Wind 2

Time: 23.08
Date: 23.7.2015

***I can hear the **thunder**,
I can see the **rain**,
I can feel its **promises**, it's healing all my **pain**.***

~

I can see the **trees,** but I can also feel the _wind,_
I can feel it blowing through my **veins**, and down my **skin**.

I can feel the **wonders,
I can see the **light**,
It's time for me to pick myself back up, and say **goodnight**.**

~

I can see the future,
I'm a singer on a stage,
Pouring my heart out to an audience; this feels strange.

~This _wind_ has me **moving**,
I can feel its every beat,
1.2.3.4, I'm moving my feet.~

~

The rain starts to pour, as I stand there so coldly,
My **body** and **mind** are no longer **depressed** and **lonely**.

Advice

Time: 05:11
Date: 24.4.2015

~

*I will give you _advice_,
But, it's up to you to take it.*

You can **listen** and **learn**,
Take life **lessons**, but don't **fake** it.

~

**In life, there are decisions,
There's **frustrations**,
But, you can **make it**.**

**Sit back and take a stop,
Look at your life; come on, let's change it.**

Promises
Time: 01:49
Date: 30.4.2015

Why do some people never know how to keep a *promise*?
The best thing in life is to try and be **honest**.

~

**Yes you Thomas,
You did not find me in a bushy fucking **forest**,
I am not some piece of **jewellery** that you can sit down
and just **polish**.**

~So why be **dishonest**?
You think that you can buy me, then just treat me like a
novice?
Dressing up and going out, acting like you're the fucking
hottest,
Come on **Thomas**.~

~

I am not an **idiot**,
As a matter of fact I am a **Goddess.**

**So, I will be on my way now,
No more eating out of your rich **pockets**,
You're so stupid, **Thomas**.**

A Good Parent
Time: 02:18
Date: 27.4.2015

~

Sometimes when you're **talking,
You don't realise who your words are **affecting**,
How can we bond, if it's only **drugs,** that you're
injecting?**

A person like you, should only know about **respecting**,
But, I am not enough, because it's men that you're
selecting.

~

What have I done *__God__*?
Please, start your **correcting**,
I am only **young**, but I need some **directing**.

***Life is so hard, I need some real **protecting**,
I better stop now, it's time to start my **reflecting**.***

Are You Ready?

Time: 23:14
Date: 6.4.2015

We are one,
We are many,
We are humans,
We are ready.

~

So hold **steady,
Life is a **journey**,
We can travel it, but let's be **ready**.**

Have no **doubt**, no **hesitation**,
Have a *clear heart,* never make it **heavy**.

~

~I know you miss **Freddy**,
But stop blaming others; this is all just stupid and **petty**.
If you want to let the tears out, then go and hold your
bloody **teddy**.~

So, let's think, **READY!**
Are you **ready**?
This is your future now, big **Eddie**.

~

*****Because, you are one,**
You are many,
You are a human,
And you are ready,
So come on, Eddie.***

I Remain
Time: 11:32
Date: 9.3.2015

~

~If you go, and I *remain*,
I will **ensure**, that I remember you **Jane**.~

If you go first, and I *remain*,
I will continue our **journey**, on the **longest trains**.

~

**If you go first, and I *remain*,
I will sell our **houses**, then go to **Spain**.**

If you go, and I *remain*,
I will **inject** your blood, through my deepest **veins**.

~

If your go first, and I *remain*,
How will I ever live, with this **pain**?

**If you go first, and I *remain*,
Then let our memory of love, **refrain**.**

Prevail

Time: 1:06
Date: 26.7.2015

The *difference* between the impossible and the possible
lies in a persons
determination.*

~

Say you **determined** that your life will **fail,**
You have just robbed a store and got caught,
Now, you will never get **bail**.

Let's just say, you're a big fat person, stepping on a **scale**,
You're **frustrated,**
You're **shaking,**
Your face is going **pale**.

~

Now, let's look at these hard ass **criminals, who never
leave a **trail**,
Do you think that they're thinking about the *impossible*? **
NO!
They just wear a **veil.**

And even though they know that their actions will put
them into **jail**,
All they do is take a breathe, breathe in, then **exhale**.

~

~So those of you, who are out there **weighing** on a **scale**,
And those of you, who are out there **waiting** to get **bail**,
Please think about an infant baby, who is now a **male**,
It took him sometime to walk, that's only because he
prevailed.~

?

Time: 23:09
Date: 28.7.2015

~

~What is your **inspiration**?
What is it that keeps you **going**?
What is it that makes you **think**?
What is it that makes you **wonder**?
What is it that _keeps_ your mind **flowing**?~

What is it that lifts you **up**?
What is it that _brings_ you **down**?
What is it that puts a smile on your **face**?
What is it that makes you **frown**?

~

What is your **motivation?
What _pushes_ you to do **more**?
What is it that makes you **laugh**?
What are the things that you **adore**?**

When you ask yourself all of these **questions**,
It **breaks** your life down into **figures**,
It makes you _realise_ what's important in **life**,
It makes you see why anger **triggers**.

~

It opens up the doors to **success**,
It frees your **creative mind**,
It gives you ways in which you can **progress**,
It encourages you to _deliver_ on **time**.

50

Better Life
2011

* It didn't take a _baby_ to **save me**,
Money can't **change me**,
I have to give **thanks** to the people that **raised me.** *

~

**Grew up in the slavery, thought about it daily,
My daddy said, "Don't worry, because everything
is gravy."**

I have to make my **money**
And, I have to make it **good**,
Because, no matter what, I ain't staying in the **hood**.

~

~ May the Lord be with me, throughout all my **days**.
Please guide and **protect me**,
And I will forever give you **praise**. ~

The Situation
Time: 09:05
Date: 31.8.2013

She said,
"She's on her way to the **doctors**,
This is it now, she **wonders**,
Is this the right thing to do?
Does he love me? I have no **clue**.

~

"I am _hurt_ NO, I can't do **this**,
He tells me how much, I am **useless**.

"I am buried in the **ground**,
All my **sins** will oneday be **found**.

~

"I am _**lost**_,
I **don't** know what to **do**,
God, I need you to help me **through**,
All this **pain**, **drama** and **anguish**,
I really can't take this **madness**.

"I am a human, just like **you**,
You have a baby, with me **too**,
I have known you for so **long**,
But I really thought that I was **strong**.

~

"All you do is break me **down**,
My _soul,_ will never be **found**,
Her mother tells her don't do it,
He will use you and _leave_ you **toothless**."

*But she loves him, so only time will **tell**,
God only knows, that this shit **smells**.*

~

He's a **player** and that's no **doubt**,
Sleeping with 3 girls, was a **crowd**.

All of them **_pregnant,_** at the **_same time,_**
Within 5 months, now that's a **crime**.

~But, who is he to really give a damn?
He has no **soul**, just like his **pants**.~

~

What about his mind; is that what the girls are **after**?
This will definitely end in a **disaster**.

He's never worked a day in his life,
He will be a player, throughout his nights.

~

***This is a real story, not just some **words**,
Read between the lines, there is no **curse**.***

B.T.L.G

Time: 22.26
Date: 28.7.2015

You don't always need a plan.

~

*Sometimes, you just need to **breathe**,
Trust,
Let go,
And see what **happens**.*

Trusting and **believing** in yourself, will always lead to
doubts,
But, as long as you know what you are working **towards**,
You can always build that **house**.

~

~Using **imagination** as one of your **strengths** will make
you worry less about **tomorrow**,
But, you have to live today as it comes even if there might
be **sorrows**.~

When you learn to **breathe**,
That's your way of saying, YES, **I can**.
When you **trust**,
That's your way of saying, God has a **plan**.

~

***When you **let go**,
That's your way of saying _negativity_, you are **banned**,
And when _success_ **happens**,
You will realise that you were a **wise man.*****

So remember to **breathe**,
Trust and always let go,
Even if you are **fighting** to be on the greatest **TV show**.

Pretty Lady
Time: 10:31
Date: 9.3.2015

~

Why are you **embarrassed**, if you don't fit in the **crowd**?
Your belly rolls is something that you should feel **proud**
off, not **doubt**.

So what, if she's **skinny?
So what, if she's **pretty**?
Do you even know if she fits in well in the **city**?**

~

~Now, you're feeling nervous and having more **doubts**,
Acting like you're too fat to get out of the **house**.~

So are you going to let them kick you **down**?
Girl, you better stop it, go stand your fucking **ground**.

~

*If it makes you feel any better, then go and lose a few
pounds,
But, don't you ever let them get you **down**.*

The Abuser
Time: 03:09
Date: 8.8.2015

You have **beaten,
You have **bruised**,
You have **abused,**
And you have **used**.**

~

How does it feel?
You have been **defused**,
Your **cord** has been **unplugged**,
You are now, **excused**.

You are staring in my face, acting like you're **confused**,
This is how it feels, when you try to **misuse**.

~

The light is no longer bright in your face, you're **diffused**,
Aww now look,
The _abuser,_ has now been _abused_.

What goes around will come back around, forget being
accused,
You always _run_ away to cool off on your **cruise**,
But, as you're sitting there, drinking up all your **booze**,
Remember that Jesus, is not very **amused**.

~

So if you think that you can sail through life and **reuse**,
People like you, will always be put to **snooze**.

Friendship
Time 00:14
Date: 17.4.2012

Happy birthday my **dear**.
I wish you all the **best**, as time, moves **near**.

~

The perfect friend, and a crazy one too,
Yes, you annoy me at times,
But, you've always stayed true.

~ I know that our *friendship* was meant to be,
Because, you were my long lost *friend*,
You were **there** for me.~

~

When I think about my life **sometimes**,
It's **amazing** how times **flies**.

But, to know that you are **here**,
I don't mind getting **older**, as time moves **near.**

~

Now, I just want to give God **thanks**.
Because I know that he has a **plan**.
A plan for you and me,
A plan, that will finally set us **free**.

Angel Dust

Time: 02:03
Date: 8.8.2015

~

I can see your words turning into **fairy dust,
All your **lying** and your **cheating**, it's an absolute
disgust.**

Yes, I loved you so **much**,
But, I knew it was **lust**,
You looked me straight in the eye, and I felt **deceit** and
distrust.

~

*All your sexual fantasies, always made me **buss**,
But, the hurt and pain, could no longer be **discussed**.*

I thought you were the person that I could always **trust**,
But, I've got my *health* and I'm *alive*, no need to kick up a
fuss.

~

~I've moved on, I have **forgiven**,
I've got the earth on my **crust**,
Yes, I've met Mr Right, and he's signed the deed of **trust**.~

***I will never miss place, or even try to get **lost**,
Because, I know the world is **floating** around in **angel
dust**.***

Death?

Time: 21:27
Date: 08.10.2015

~I want to know what happens after **death**,
That moment when you close your eyes and take your last
breath.~

~

Please can I know what happens after **death**?
That moment when you get shot,
Is there any more **stress**?

We all want to know what happens after **death**,
We live, to learn, to see if life is a **test.**

~

But, no one really knows what happens after **death**,
Does that feeling in your gut tell you that you will be **next**?

We can never know what happens after **death**,
Until it is our turn, we have to live our lives, and do our
best.

Cheaters Choice

Time: 02:44
Date: 8.8.2015

~

~Losing you, has been my greatest ever **achievement**.~

All the **pain**,
Drama,
And **anguish**,
But, most of all, the **disappointments**.

~

*When a **cheater** has realised that he's been played and no
longer the **cheat**,
His body gets locked up into **confinement**.*

His brain shuts **down**,
He can no longer wear his **crown**,
He's broken and cannot take all the **excitement**.

~

To you, every other girl was an **assignment**.

~You **abused** them,
You **used** them,
Lock them away and **accused** them,
Only to turn them over for another man to refine them.~

~

But, now you've been hurt, you're feeling **lost**,
Your money came at a **cost**,
Next time, you should think about how you make your
next **appointments**.

Not all girls are the **same,
Some of them plays, the men **games**,
So, think twice before you choose your **employment****

Temptation
Time: 00:05
Date: 26.7.2015

~

It will take **sometime,
Yes, it will take some **motivation**,
It will require **sacrifice**,
And, it will lead to **frustration**.**

There are going to be times when you will feel the
temptation,
But, I promise you this,
Life is about, **determination**.

~

~You might get an *invitation,* to go and some **weed**,
They will let you sit **down**,
And watch you, while you **bleed**.~

There are going to be days when that alcoholic drink is
looking at you saying,
"I'm your **seed**,
You know you wanna drink me baby,
let's **proceed**"

~

*But, if you want to **succeed**,
Please take the time out and just listen to this _message,_ I
would never **mislead***.

This is your **life**,
This is your **time**,
Stay focus, think about that baby that you need to **feed**.

A negative mind, will never understand how to live a positive future.

Printed in March 2023
by Rotomail Italia S.p.A., Vignate (MI) - Italy